B

To

Lepiy – Who has
become such
From   a wonderful
                    young
Nana – Elaine Lady

BroadStreet Publishing Group, LLC.
Racine, Wisconsin, U.S.A
Broadstreetpublishing.com

BIBLE PROMISES OF
Comfort and Encouragement

ISBN 978-1-4245-4995-5

Compiled by Michelle Winger | literallyprecise.com
Designed by Chris Garborg | garborgdesign.com

Printed in China

BIBLE PROMISES

OF
Comfort AND
Encouragement

BroadStreet
PUBLISHING

*E*veryone experiences difficult seasons in life. Loss, pain, anxiety, and frustration can lead to discouragement and sometimes a feeling of hopelessness. *Bible Promises of Comfort and Encouragement* is a topically organized collection of Scripture that is designed to help you receive the assurance and inspiration found in the promises of God's Word.

Each theme shares Bible promises that encourage you to reflect on who God is, and what He wants to be for you, in your moments of struggle.

Take comfort and encouragement in the promises of God today.

—CONTENTS—

Ability

"My grace is sufficient for you, for my power is made perfect in weakness." Therefore I will boast all the more gladly of my weaknesses, so that the power of Christ may rest upon me.

2 CORINTHIANS 12:9 ESV

After you have suffered for a little while, the God of all grace, who called you to His eternal glory in Christ, will Himself perfect, confirm, strengthen and establish you.

1 PETER 5:10 NASB

Take a new grip with your tired hands and strengthen your weak knees. Mark out a straight path for your feet so that those who are weak and lame will not fall but become strong.

HEBREWS 12:12-13 NLT

We can rejoice, too, when we run into problems and trials, for we know that they help us develop endurance. And endurance develops strength of character, and character strengthens our confident hope of salvation. And this hope will not lead to disappointment. For we know how dearly God loves us, because he has given us the Holy Spirit to fill our hearts with his love.

ROMANS 5:3–5 NLT

We are not saying that we can do this work ourselves. It is God who makes us able to do all that we do.

2 CORINTHIANS 3:5 NCV

Acceptance

I've redeemed you.

I've called your name. You're mine.

When you're in over your head, I'll be there with you.

When you're in rough waters, you will not go down.

When you're between a rock and a hard place,

it won't be a dead end—

Because I am GOD, your personal God,

The Holy of Israel, your Savior.

I paid a huge price for you...!

That's how much you mean to me!

That's how much I love you!

ISAIAH 43:1–4 MSG

If God is for us, who can be against us?

ROMANS 8:31 ESV

The Father gives me the people who are mine.

Every one of them will come to me,

and I will always accept them.

JOHN 6:37 NCV

Here I am! I stand at the door and knock.

If anyone hears my voice and opens the door,

I will come in and eat with that person,

and they with me.

REVELATION 3:20 NIV

Before he made the world, God chose us to be

his very own through what Christ would do for us;

he decided then to make us holy in his eyes,

without a single fault—we who stand before

him covered with his love.

EPHESIANS 1:4 TLB

Adoption

You did not receive a spirit of slavery to fall back into fear, but you have received a spirit of adoption. When we cry, "Abba! Father!" it is that very Spirit bearing witness with our spirit that we are children of God.

ROMANS 8:15–16 NRSV

A father of the fatherless and a judge for the widows,
Is God in His holy habitation.
God makes a home for the lonely;
He leads out the prisoners into prosperity.

PSALM 68:5-6 NASB

I will not abandon you as orphans—
I will come to you.

JOHN 14:18 NLT

I will bring the blind by a way they did not know;
I will lead them in paths they have not known.
I will make darkness light before them,
And crooked places straight.
These things will I do for them,
And not forsake them.

ISAIAH 42:16 NKJV

The LORD will not abandon His people on account
of His great name, because the LORD has been
pleased to make you a people for Himself.

1 SAMUEL 12:22 NASB

But when the right time came, God sent his Son, born
of a woman, subject to the law. God sent him to buy
freedom for us who were slaves to the law, so that he
could adopt us as his very own children.

GALATIANS 4:4-5 NLT

Affection

I am my beloved's,

And his desire is toward me.

SONG OF SOLOMON 7:10 NKJV

You make known to me the path of life;

you will fill me with joy in your presence,

with eternal pleasures at your right hand.

PSALM 16:11 NIV

It's in Christ that we find out who we are and what we are living for. Long before we first heard of Christ and got our hopes up, he had his eye on us, had designs on us for glorious living, part of the overall purpose he is working out in everything and everyone.

EPHESIANS 1:11–12 MSG

My beloved speaks and says to me:
"Arise, my love, my beautiful one,
and come away,
for behold, the winter is past;
the rain is over and gone.
The flowers appear on the earth,
the time of singing has come."

Song of Solomon 2:10-12 esv

The LORD your God is living among you.
He is a mighty savior.
He will take delight in you with gladness.
With his love, he will calm all your fears.
He will rejoice over you with joyful songs.

Zephaniah 3:17 nlt

My God is changeless in his love for me,
and he will come and help me.

Psalm 59:10 tlb

Assurance

The LORD always keeps his promises;
he is gracious in all he does.

PSALM 145:13 NLT

He has granted to us his precious and very great
promises, so that through them you may become
partakers of the divine nature, having escaped from
the corruption that is in the world.

2 PETER 1:3-4 ESV

Your promises have been thoroughly tested,
and your servant loves them.
...My eyes stay open through the watches of the night,
that I may meditate on your promises.

PSALM 119:140, 148 NIV

To him who is able to do immeasurably more than all
we ask or imagine, according to his power that is at
work within us, to him be glory...for ever and ever!
Amen.

EPHESIANS 3:20–21 NIV

All of God's promises have been fulfilled
in Christ with a resounding "Yes!"

2 CORINTHIANS 1:20 NLT

Jesus Christ is the same yesterday and
today and forever.

HEBREWS 13:8 NASB

These things I have written to you who believe
in the name of the Son of God, that you may know
that you have eternal life, and that you may continue
to believe in the name of the Son of God.

1 JOHN 5:13 NKJV

Authenticity

If you're content to simply be yourself,
your life will count for plenty.

MATTHEW 23:12 MSG

It's who you are and the way you live that count
before God. Your worship must engage your spirit
in the pursuit of truth. That's the kind of people the
Father is out looking for: those who are simply and
honestly *themselves* before him in their worship.
God is sheer being itself—Spirit. Those who worship
him must do it out of their very being, their spirits,
their true selves, in adoration.

JOHN 4:23–24 MSG

Take your everyday, ordinary life—your sleeping, eating, going-to-work, and walking-around life— and place it before God as an offering. Embracing what God does for you is the best thing you can do for him. Don't become so well-adjusted to your culture that you fit into it without even thinking. Instead, fix your attention on God. You'll be changed from the inside out. Readily recognize what he wants from you, and quickly respond to it. Unlike the culture around you, always dragging you down to its level of immaturity, God brings the best out of you, develops well-formed maturity in you.

ROMANS 12:1–2 MSG

Blessing

Blessed be the God and Father of our Lord Jesus
Christ, who has blessed us in Christ with every
spiritual blessing in the heavenly places, even as he
chose us in him before the foundation of the world,
that we should be holy and blameless before him.

EPHESIANS 1:3–4 ESV

You prepare a feast for me
in the presence of my enemies.
You honor me by anointing my head with oil.
My cup overflows with blessings.

PSALM 23:5 NLT

From his abundance we have all received one gracious
blessing after another.

JOHN 1:16 NLT

The LORD bless you, and keep you;
The LORD make His face shine on you,
And be gracious to you;
The LORD lift up His countenance on you,
And give you peace.

NUMBERS 6:24–26 NASB

How blessed all those in whom you live,
whose lives become roads you travel;
They wind through lonesome valleys, come upon brooks,
discover cool springs and pools brimming with rain!

PSALM 84:5–6 MSG

For the LORD God is our sun and our shield.
He gives us grace and glory.
The LORD will withhold no good thing
from those who do what is right.

PSALM 84:11 NLT

Boldness

Let us therefore come boldly to the throne of grace,
that we may obtain mercy and find grace to
help in time of need.

HEBREWS 4:16 NKJV

In all this you greatly rejoice, though now for a
little while you may have had to suffer grief in all
kinds of trials. These have come so that the proven
genuineness of your faith—of greater worth than
gold, which perishes even though refined by fire—
may result in praise, glory and honor when
Jesus Christ is revealed.

1 PETER 1:6–7 NIV

We are pressed on every side by troubles,
but we are not crushed. We are perplexed,
but not driven to despair. We are hunted down,
but never abandoned by God. We get knocked down,
but we are not destroyed.

2 Corinthians 4:8–9 nlt

If you're serious about living this new resurrection
life with Christ, *act* like it. Pursue the things over
which Christ presides. Don't shuffle along,
eyes to the ground, absorbed with the things
right in front of you. Look up, and be alert to what is
going on around Christ—that's where the action is.
See things from *his* perspective.

Colossians 3:1–2 msg

Comfort

May your unfailing love be my comfort,
according to your promise to your servant.

Psalm 119:76 NIV

God's dwelling place is now among the people,
and he will dwell with them.... "He will wipe every
tear from their eyes. There will be no more death"
or mourning or crying or pain, for the old order
of things has passed away.

Revelation 21:3–4 NIV

May our Lord Jesus Christ himself and God our
Father, who loved us and by his grace gave us
eternal comfort and a wonderful hope,
comfort you and strengthen you.

2 Thessalonians 2:16–17 NLT

Unless the LORD had helped me,
I would soon have settled in the silence of the grave.
I cried out, "I am slipping!"
but your unfailing love, O LORD, supported me.
When doubts filled my mind,
your comfort gave me renewed hope and cheer.

PSALM 94:17–19 NLT

Praise be to the God and Father of our
Lord Jesus Christ, the Father of compassion
and the God of all comfort.

2 CORINTHIANS 1:3 NIV

To all who mourn...he will give: beauty for ashes;
joy instead of mourning; praise instead of heaviness.
For God has planted them like strong and
graceful oaks for his own glory.

ISAIAH 61:3 TLB

Compassion

You, O Lord,

are a God full of compassion, and gracious,

Longsuffering and abundant in mercy and truth.

PSALM 86:15 NKJV

Blessed be the God…of all comfort, who comforts us
in all our tribulation, that we may be able to comfort
those who are in any trouble, with the comfort with
which we ourselves are comforted by God.

2 CORINTHIANS 1:3–4 NKJV

Let love be without hypocrisy. Abhor what is evil.
Cling to what is good. Be kindly affectionate to one
another with brotherly love.

ROMANS 12:9–10 NKJV

When she speaks, her words are wise,
and she gives instructions with kindness.

PROVERBS 31:26 NLT

Be kind and compassionate to one another.

EPHESIANS 4:32 NIV

How does God's love abide in anyone who has the
world's goods and sees a brother or sister in need and
yet refuses help? Little children, let us love, not in
word or speech, but in truth and action.

1 JOHN 3:17–18 NRSV

As those who have been chosen of God, holy and
beloved, put on a heart of compassion, kindness,
humility, gentleness and patience…. Beyond all these
things put on love, which is the perfect bond of unity.

COLOSSIANS 3:12, 14 NASB

Composure

Don't worry about anything; instead, pray about
everything. Tell God what you need, and thank him
for all he has done. Then you will experience God's
peace, which exceeds anything we can understand.
His peace will guard your hearts and minds as
you live in Christ Jesus.

PHILIPPIANS 4:6–7 NLT

Worry weighs a person down;
an encouraging word cheers a person up.

PROVERBS 12:25 NLT

Which of you by worrying can add
a single hour to his life's span?

LUKE 12:25 NASB

Give your burdens to the LORD,
and he will take care of you.

PSALM 55:22 NLT

Do not worry about your life, what you will eat or
drink; or about your body, what you will wear.
Is not life more than food, and the body more than
clothes? Look at the birds of the air; they do not
sow or reap or store away in barns, and yet your
heavenly Father feeds them. Are you not much
more valuable than they?

MATTHEW 6:25–26 NIV

May the Lord of peace himself give you
peace at all times in every way.

2 THESSALONIANS 3:16 ESV

If people's thinking is controlled by the sinful self,
there is death. But if their thinking is controlled by
the Spirit, there is life and peace.

ROMANS 8:6 NCV

Confidence

I can do everything through Christ,
who gives me strength.

PHILIPPIANS 4:13 NLT

This is the confidence that we have toward him, that if
we ask anything according to his will he hears us. And if
we know that he hears us in whatever we ask, we know
that we have the requests that we have asked of him.

1 JOHN 5:14–15 ESV

Let us then approach God's throne of grace with
confidence, so that we may receive mercy and find
grace to help us in our time of need.

HEBREWS 4:16 NIV

Be my rock of refuge,

to which I can always go;

give the command to save me,

for you are my rock and my fortress....

You have been my hope, Sovereign Lord,

my confidence since my youth.

Psalm 71:3, 5 niv

We can confidently say, "The Lord is my helper;

I will not fear; what can man do to me?"

Hebrews 13:6 esv

I am confident of this very thing,

that He who began a good work in you

will perfect it until the day of Christ Jesus.

Philippians 1:6 nasb

But if you remain in me and my words

remain in you, you may ask for anything

you want, and it will be granted!

John 15:7 nlt

Consolation

You, O LORD, are a shield about me,
My glory, and the One who lifts my head.

Blessed be the LORD,
Because He has heard the voice of my supplication.
The LORD is my strength and my shield;
My heart trusts in Him, and I am helped;
Therefore my heart exults,
And with my song I shall thank Him.

PSALM 28:6-7 NASB

He turned my sorrow into joy!
He took away my clothes of mourning
and clothed me with joy.

PSALM 30:11 TLB

Gladness and joy will overtake them,

and sorrow and sighing will flee away.

ISAIAH 35:10 NIV

Those that the LORD has rescued will return.

They will enter Zion with singing;

everlasting joy will crown their heads.

He did rescue us from mortal danger, and he will

rescue us again. We have placed our confidence in

him, and he will continue to rescue us.

2 CORINTHIANS 1:10 NLT

He will once again fill your mouth with laughter

and your lips with shouts of joy.

JOB 8:21 NLT

The LORD longs to be gracious to you;

therefore he will rise up to show you compassion.

For the LORD is a God of justice.

Blessed are all who wait for him!

ISAIAH 30:18 NIV

Contentment

I know what it is to be in need, and I know what it
is to have plenty. I have learned the secret of being
content in any and every situation, whether well fed
or hungry, whether living in plenty or in want. I can
do all this through him who gives me strength.

PHILIPPIANS 4:12-13 NIV

Oh, how sweet the light of day,
and how wonderful to live in the sunshine!
Even if you live a long time,
don't take a single day for granted.
Take delight in each light-filled hour.

ECCLESIASTES 11:7–8 MSG

You're blessed when you're content with just
who you are—no more, no less. That's the
moment you find yourselves proud owners
of everything that can't be bought.

MATTHEW 5:5 MSG

If God cares so wonderfully for wildflowers
that are here today and thrown into the fire
tomorrow, he will certainly care for you. Why do you
have so little faith? So don't worry about these things,
saying, "What will we eat? What will we drink?
What will we wear?" These things dominate the
thoughts of unbelievers, but your heavenly Father
already knows all your needs. Seek the Kingdom of
God above all else, and live righteously, and he will
give you everything you need.

MATTHEW 6:30-33 NLT

Courage

Be strong and courageous. Do not be frightened, and
do not be dismayed, for the Lord your God is with
you wherever you go.

Joshua 1:9 esv

Love the Lord, all you godly ones!
For the Lord protects those who are loyal to him,
but he harshly punishes the arrogant.
So be strong and courageous,
all you who put your hope in the Lord!

Psalm 31:23–24 nlt

When I am afraid, I put my trust in you.
In God, whose word I praise—
in God I trust and am not afraid.

Psalm 56:3–4 niv

Even though I walk through the valley

of the shadow of death,

I fear no evil, for You are with me;

Your rod and Your staff, they comfort me.

PSALM 23:4 NASB

May he give you the power to accomplish all the good

things your faith prompts you to do.

2 THESSALONIANS 1:11 NLT

Be on guard. Stand firm in the faith. Be courageous.

Be strong. And do everything with love.

1 CORINTHIANS 16:13–14 NLT

I eagerly expect and hope that I will in no way be

ashamed, but will have sufficient courage so that now

as always Christ will be exalted in my body, whether

by life or by death.

PHILIPPIANS 1:20 NIV

Delight

Enter his gates with thanksgiving,
and his courts with praise.
Give thanks to him, bless his name.
For the LORD is good;
his steadfast love endures forever,
and his faithfulness to all generations.

PSALM 100:4–5 NRSV

He will yet fill your mouth with laughter
and your lips with shouts of joy.

JOB 8:21 NIV

The Lord has done great things for us,
and we are filled with joy.

PSALM 126:3 NIV

May you be filled with joy, always thanking the
Father. He has enabled you to share in the inheritance
that belongs to his people, who live in the light.

COLOSSIANS 1:11–12 NLT

Happy are those who hear the joyful call to worship,
for they will walk in the light of your presence, LORD.

PSALM 89:15 NLT

Rejoice in the Lord always. Again I will say, rejoice!

PHILIPPIANS 4:4 NKJV

I know that there is nothing better for people than to
be happy and to do good while they live.

ECCLESIASTES 3:12 NIV

I will give thanks to the LORD with my whole heart;
I will recount all of your wonderful deeds.
I will be glad and exult in you;
I will sing praise to your name, O Most High.

PSALM 9:1-2 ESV

Deliverance

The LORD hears his people when they call to him for help.
He rescues them from all their troubles.

PSALM 34:17 NLT

I waited patiently for the LORD;
he turned to me and heard my cry.
He lifted me out of the slimy pit,
out of the mud and mire;
he set my feet on a rock
and gave me a firm place to stand.
He put a new song in my mouth,
a hymn of praise to our God.
Many will see and fear the LORD;
and put their trust in him.

PSALM 40:1–3 NIV

Humble yourselves in the sight of the Lord,
and He will lift you up.

JAMES 4:10 NKJV

My prayer is to you, O LORD.
At an acceptable time, O God,
in the abundance of your steadfast love
answer me in your saving faithfulness.
Deliver me
from sinking in the mire;
let me be delivered from my enemies
and from the deep waters.
Answer me, O LORD, for your steadfast love is good;
according to your abundant mercy, turn to me.

PSALM 69:13-14, 16 ESV

The righteous person faces many troubles,
but the LORD comes to the rescue each time.

PSALM 34:19 NLT

Devotion

Commit everything you do to the LORD.
Trust him, and he will help you.

PSALM 37:5 NLT

Stand firm. Let nothing move you. Always give
yourselves fully to the work of the Lord, because you
know that your labor in the Lord is not in vain.

1 CORINTHIANS 15:58 NIV

With all my heart I have sought You;
Do not let me wander from Your commandments.
Your word I have treasured in my heart,
That I may not sin against You.
...Teach me, O LORD, the way of Your statutes,
And I shall observe it to the end.

PSALM 119:10–11, 33 NASB

If any of you wants to be my follower,
you must turn from your selfish ways,
take up your cross daily, and follow me.

Luke 9:23 nlt

Commit your work to the LORD,
and your plans will be established.

Proverbs 16:3 esv

Seek first the kingdom of God and His righteousness,
and all these things shall be added to you.

Matthew 6:33 nkjv

May God himself, the God of peace, sanctify you
through and through. May your whole spirit, soul
and body be kept blameless at the coming of our Lord
Jesus Christ. The one who calls you is faithful,
and he will do it.

1 Thessalonians 5:23–24 niv

Encouragement

The humble will see their God at work and be glad.
Let all who seek God's help be encouraged.

PSALM 69:32 NLT

We do not lose heart, but though our outer man is
decaying, yet our inner man is being renewed day
by day. For momentary, light affliction is producing
for us an eternal weight of glory far beyond all
comparison.

2 CORINTHIANS 4:16–17 NASB

Let us consider how to stir up one another to love and
good works, not neglecting to meet together, as is the
habit of some, but encouraging one another.

HEBREWS 10:24–25 ESV

Though an army besiege me,

my heart will not fear;

though war break out against me,

even then I will be confident.

One thing I ask from the LORD,

this only do I seek:

that I may dwell in the house of the LORD

all the days of my life,

to gaze on the beauty of the LORD

and to seek him in his temple.

For in the day of trouble

he will keep me safe in his dwelling.

PSALM 27:3-5 NIV

May the God who gives endurance and
encouragement give you the same attitude of mind
toward each other that Christ Jesus had.

ROMANS 15:5 NIV

Enrichment

Oh, the depth of the riches both of the wisdom
and knowledge of God! How unsearchable are His
judgments and unfathomable His ways!

ROMANS 11:33 NASB

Blessed are those who find wisdom,
those who gain understanding,
for she is more profitable than silver
and yields better returns than gold.
She is more precious than rubies;
nothing you desire can compare with her.
Long life is in her right hand;
in her left hand are riches and honor.
Her ways are pleasant ways,
and all her paths are peace.

PROVERBS 3:13–17 NIV

A good man's speech reveals the
rich treasures within him.

MATTHEW 12:35 TLB

Every good gift and every perfect gift is from above,
coming down from the Father of lights with whom
there is no variation or shadow due to change.

JAMES 1:17 ESV

I will tell of the kindnesses of the LORD,
the deeds for which he is to be praised,
according to all the LORD has done for us…
according to his compassion and many kindnesses.

ISAIAH 63:7 NIV

Everything God created is good, and nothing is to be
rejected if it is received with thanksgiving.

1 TIMOTHY 4:4 NIV

GOD's blessing makes life rich;
nothing we do can improve on God.

PROVERBS 10:22 MSG

Eternity

I will come back and take you to be with me
that you also may be where I am.

John 14:3 niv

We fix our eyes not on what is seen,
but on what is unseen, since what is seen is
temporary, but what is unseen is eternal.

2 Corinthians 4:18 niv

Before the mountains were brought forth,
or ever you had formed the earth and the world,
from everlasting to everlasting you are God.

Psalm 90:2 esv.

We are citizens of heaven, where the Lord Jesus Christ lives. And we are eagerly waiting for him to return as our Savior. He will take our weak mortal bodies and change them into glorious bodies like his own, using the same power with which he will bring everything under his control.

PHILIPPIANS 3:20–21 NLT

Surely goodness and mercy shall follow me
All the days of my life;
And I will dwell in the house of the LORD
Forever.

PSALM 23:6 NKJV

I'm asking GOD for one thing,
only one thing:
To live with him in his house
my whole life long.
I'll contemplate his beauty;
I'll study at his feet.

PSALM 27:4 MSG

Faith

Faith is confidence in what we hope for
and assurance about what we do not see.

HEBREWS 11:1 NIV

Through Christ you have come to trust in God. And
you have placed your faith and hope in God because he
raised Christ from the dead and gave him great glory.

1 PETER 1:21 NLT

Not one word of all the good words which the LORD
your God spoke concerning you has failed; all have
been fulfilled for you, not one of them has failed.

JOSHUA 23:14 NASB

Faith comes by hearing, and hearing
by the word of God.

Romans 10:17 nkjv

If you have faith like a grain of mustard seed, you will
say to this mountain, "Move from here to there," and
it will move, and nothing will be impossible for you.

Matthew 17:20 esv

As we pray to our God and Father about you, we think of
your faithful work, your loving deeds, and the enduring
hope you have because of our Lord Jesus Christ.

1 Thessalonians 1:3 nlt

Until heaven and earth disappear,
not the smallest letter, not the least stroke of a pen,
will by any means disappear from the Law until
everything is accomplished.

Matthew 5:18 niv

Faithfulness

Let us draw near to God with a sincere heart
and with the full assurance that faith brings....
Let us hold unswervingly to the hope we profess,
for he who promised is faithful.

LORD, you are my God;
I will exalt you and praise your name,
for in perfect faithfulness
you have done wonderful things,
things planned long ago.

ISAIAH 25:1 NIV

Your lovingkindness, O LORD, extends to the heavens,
Your faithfulness reaches to the skies.

PSALM 36:5 NASB

Be attentive to my words;

incline your ear to my sayings.

Let them not escape from your sight;

keep them within your heart.

Let your eyes look directly forward,

and your gaze be straight before you.

PROVERBS 4:20–21, 25 ESV

God is faithful. He will not allow the temptation to be more than you can stand. When you are tempted, he will show you a way out so that you can endure.

1 CORINTHIANS 10:13 NLT

The word of the LORD is upright,

and all his work is done in faithfulness.

PSALM 33:4 ESV

I keep my eyes always on the LORD.

With him at my right hand, I will not be shaken.

PSALM 16:8 NIV

Fearlessness

Don't be afraid, for I am with you.

Don't be discouraged, for I am your God.

I will strengthen you and help you.

I will hold you up with my victorious right hand.

ISAIAH 41:10 NLT

God has not given us a spirit of fear, but of power and

of love and of a sound mind.

2 TIMOTHY 1:7 NKJV

The LORD is my light and my salvation;

whom shall I fear?

The LORD is the stronghold of my life;

of whom shall I be afraid?

PSALM 27:1 ESV

There is no room in love for fear.

Well-formed love banishes fear. Since fear is crippling,

a fearful life—fear of death, fear of judgment—

is one not yet fully formed in love.

1 John 4:18 msg

When you lie down, you will not be afraid;

when you lie down, your sleep will be sweet.

Have no fear of sudden disaster

or of the ruin that overtakes the wicked,

for the Lord will be at your side

and will keep your foot from being snared.

Proverbs 3:24–26 niv

Say to those with fearful hearts,

"Be strong, and do not fear,

for your God…is coming to save you."

Isaiah 35:4 nlt

Forgiveness

He is so rich in kindness and grace that
he purchased our freedom with the blood of
his Son and forgave our sins.

EPHESIANS 1:7 NLT

Her sins—and they are many—have been forgiven,
so she has shown me much love. But a person who is
forgiven little shows only little love.

LUKE 7:47 NLT

If we confess our sins, He is faithful and
just to forgive us our sins and to cleanse us
from all unrighteousness.

1 JOHN 1:9 NKJV

As far as the east is from the west,
So far has He removed our transgressions from us.

PSALM 103:12 NASB

My sacrifice, O God, is a broken spirit;
a broken and contrite heart
you, God, will not despise.

PSALM 51:17 NIV

If you forgive other people when they sin against you,
your heavenly Father will also forgive you.

MATTHEW 6:14 NIV

For You, Lord, are good, and ready to forgive,
And abundant in mercy to all those who call upon You.

PSALM 86:5 NKJV

Whenever you stand praying, forgive, if you have
anything against anyone, so that your Father also
who is in heaven may forgive you.

MARK 11:25 ESV

Fortitude

Be my rock of refuge,

to which I can always go;

give the command to save me,

for you are my rock and my fortress....

You have been my hope, Sovereign LORD,

my confidence since my youth.

PSALM 71:3, 5 NIV

The LORD is my rock and my fortress

and my deliverer;

My God, my rock, in whom I take refuge,

My shield and the horn of my salvation, my

stronghold and my refuge.

2 SAMUEL 22:2-3 NASB

Lord, I trust in you alone. Don't let my
enemies defeat me. Rescue me because you are the
God who always does what is right. Answer quickly
when I cry to you; bend low and hear my whispered
plea. Be for me a great Rock of safety from my foes.
Yes, you are my Rock and my fortress.

PSALM 31:1-3 TLB

Think of what you were when you were called.
Not many of you were wise by human standards;
not many were influential; not many were of noble
birth. But God chose the foolish things of the world
to shame the wise; God chose the weak things
of the world to shame the strong.... so that
no one may boast before him.

1 CORINTHIANS 1:26-27, 29 NIV

Freedom

Jesus said, "If you hold to my teaching, you are really
my disciples. Then you will know the truth, and the
truth will set you free."

JOHN 8:31–32 NIV

Understand what we are telling you: You can have
forgiveness of your sins through Jesus. The law of
Moses could not free you from your sins. But through
Jesus everyone who believes is free from all sins.

ACTS 13:38-39 NCV

But now that you have been set free from sin and
have become slaves of God, the benefit you reap leads
to holiness, and the result is eternal life.

ROMANS 6:22 NIV

There is now no condemnation for those who are in
Christ Jesus, because through Christ Jesus
the law of the Spirit who gives life has set you free
from the law of sin and death.

ROMANS 8:1–2 NIV

He has delivered us from the power of darkness and
conveyed us into the kingdom of the Son of His love.

COLOSSIANS 1:13 NKJV

Now the Lord is the Spirit, and where the Spirit of the
Lord is, there is freedom.

2 CORINTHIANS 3:17 NRSV

So Christ has truly set us free. Now make sure
that you stay free, and don't get tied
up again in slavery to the law.

GALATIANS 5:1 NLT

Friendship

The LORD is near to all who call on him,

to all who call on him in truth.

PSALM 145:18 NIV

By this we know that we abide in Him and He in us,

because He has given us of His Spirit.

1 JOHN 4:13 NASB

Behold, I am with you always, to the end of the age.

MATTHEW 28:20 ESV

Turn to me and have mercy,

for I am alone and in deep distress.

PSALM 25:16 NLT

The amazing grace of the Master, Jesus Christ, the extravagant love of God, the intimate friendship of the Holy Spirit, be with all of you.

2 Corinthians 13:14 msg

Here I am! I stand at the door and knock. If anyone hears my voice and opens the door, I will come in and eat with that person, and they with me.

Revelation 3:20 niv

The right word at the right time
is like a custom-made piece of jewelry,
And a wise friend's timely reprimand
is like a gold ring slipped on your finger.
Reliable friends who do what they say
are like cool drinks in sweltering heat—refreshing!

Proverbs 25:12–13 msg

A friend loves at all times.

Proverbs 17:17 nkjv

Grace

Where is another God like you, who pardons the sins
of the survivors among his people? You cannot
stay angry with your people, for you love to be merciful.
Once again you will have compassion on us.
You will tread our sins beneath your feet; you will throw
them into the depths of the ocean! You will bless us as
you promised Jacob long ago. You will set your love upon
us, as you promised our father Abraham!

MICAH 7:18–20 TLB

He gives more grace. Therefore He says:
"God resists the proud,
But gives grace to the humble."

JAMES 4:6 NKJV

God is so rich in mercy, and he loved us so much, that even though we were dead because of our sins, he gave us life when he raised Christ from the dead. (It is only by God's grace that you have been saved!)… God saved you by his grace when you believed. And you can't take credit for this; it is a gift from God. Salvation is not a reward for the good things we have done, so none of us can boast about it.

EPHESIANS 2:4–5, 8–9 NLT

Sin shall no longer be your master, because you are not under the law, but under grace.

ROMANS 6:14 NIV

Guidance

We can make our plans,

but the LORD determines our steps.

PROVERBS 16:9 NLT

The true children of God are those

who let God's Spirit lead them.

ROMANS 8:14 NCV

Guide me in your truth and teach me,

for you are God my Savior,

and my hope is in you all day long.

PSALM 25:5 NIV

Whether you turn to the right or to the left,

your ears will hear a voice behind you, saying,

"This is the way; walk in it."

ISAIAH 30:21 NIV

Trust in the LORD with all your heart,

And lean not on your own understanding;

In all your ways acknowledge Him,

And He shall direct your paths.

PROVERBS 3:5–6 NKJV

We ask God to give you complete knowledge of
his will and to give you spiritual wisdom and
understanding. Then the way you live will always
honor and please the Lord, and your lives will produce
every kind of good fruit. All the while, you will grow
as you learn to know God better and better.

COLOSSIANS 1:9–10 NLT

Listen to advice and accept discipline,
and at the end you will be counted among the wise.

PROVERBS 19:20 NIV

Health

He was pierced for our transgressions,

he was crushed for our iniquities;

the punishment that brought us peace was on him,

and by his wounds we are healed.

ISAIAH 53:5 NIV

My child, pay attention to what I say.

Listen carefully to my words.

Don't lose sight of them.

Let them penetrate deep into your heart,

for they bring life to those who find them,

and healing to their whole body.

PROVERBS 4:20–22 NLT

A cheerful heart does good like medicine.

PROVERBS 17:22 TLB

Daughter, your faith has made you well;
go in peace and be healed of your affliction.

Mark 5:34 nasb

Trust God from the bottom of your heart;
don't try to figure out everything on your own.
Listen for God's voice in everything you do,
everywhere you go;
he's the one who will keep you on track.
Don't assume that you know it all.
Run to God! Run from evil!
Your body will glow with health,
your very bones will vibrate with life!

Proverbs 3:5–8 msg

The world and its desires pass away,
but whoever does the will of God lives forever.

1 John 2:17 niv

Hope

May the God of hope fill you with all joy and peace as
you trust in him, so that you may overflow with hope
by the power of the Holy Spirit.

ROMANS 15:13 NIV

The LORD is good to those whose hope is in him,
to the one who seeks him.

LAMENTATIONS 3:25 NIV

There is surely a future hope for you,
and your hope will not be cut off.

PROVERBS 23:18 NIV

We can rejoice, too, when we run into problems and
trials, for we know that they help us
develop endurance. And endurance develops strength
of character, and character strengthens our confident
hope of salvation. And this hope will not lead to
disappointment. For we know how dearly God loves
us, because he has given us the Holy Spirit to
fill our hearts with his love.

Romans 5:3–5 nlt

God…rekindles burned-out lives with fresh hope,
Restoring dignity and respect to their lives—
a place in the sun!

1 Samuel 2:7–8 msg

Blessed be the God and Father of our Lord Jesus
Christ! According to his great mercy, he has caused
us to be born again to a living hope through the
resurrection of Jesus Christ.

1 Peter 1:3 esv

Inspiration

I am the Light of the world; he who follows Me
will not walk in the darkness, but will have
the Light of life.

JOHN 8:12 NASB

The precepts of the LORD are right,
giving joy to the heart.
The commands of the LORD are radiant,
giving light to the eyes.

PSALM 19:8 NIV

Your laws are my treasure; they are my heart's delight.

PSALM 119:111 NLT

You are the light of the world. A city set on a hill cannot be hidden. Nor do people light a lamp and put it under a basket, but on a stand, and it gives light to all in the house. In the same way, let your light shine before others, so that they may see your good works and give glory to your Father who is in heaven.

MATTHEW 5:14–16 ESV

Pursue a righteous life—a life of wonder, faith, love, steadiness, courtesy. Run hard and fast in the faith. Seize the eternal life, the life you were called to, the life you so fervently embraced in the presence of so many witnesses.

1 TIMOTHY 6:11–12 MSG

I have been crucified with Christ; and it is no longer I who live, but Christ lives in me.

GALATIANS 2:20 NASB

Integrity

Show yourself in all respects to be a model of good
works, and in your teaching show integrity, dignity,
and sound speech that cannot be condemned,
so that an opponent may be put to shame,
having nothing evil to say about us.

TITUS 2:7-8 ESV

A gossip goes around telling secrets,
but those who are trustworthy can keep a confidence.

PROVERBS 11:13 NLT

One who is faithful in a very little
is also faithful in much.

LUKE 16:10 ESV

You must remain faithful to the things you have been
taught. You know they are true, for you know you can
trust those who taught you. You have been taught the
holy Scriptures from childhood, and they have given
you the wisdom to receive the salvation that comes
by trusting in Christ Jesus.

2 TIMOTHY 3:14–15 NLT

The LORD detests lying lips,
but he delights in people who are trustworthy.

PROVERBS 12:22 NIV

Love and truth form a good leader;
sound leadership is founded on loving integrity.

PROVERBS 20:28 MSG

Listen, for I will speak of excellent things,
And from the opening of my lips will come right things;
For my mouth will speak truth.

PROVERBS 8:6–7 NKJV

Intimacy

O LORD, You have searched me and known me.
You know my sitting down and my rising up;
You understand my thought afar off.
You comprehend my path and my lying down,
And are acquainted with all my ways.
For there is not a word on my tongue,
But behold, O LORD, You know it altogether.

PSALM 139:1–4 NKJV

"For I know the plans I have for you,"
declares the LORD,
"plans to prosper you and not to harm you,
plans to give you hope and a future."

JEREMIAH 29:11 NIV

When I was a child, I spoke and thought and reasoned as a child. But when I grew up, I put away childish things. Now we see things imperfectly, like puzzling reflections in a mirror, but then we will see everything with perfect clarity. All that I know now is partial and incomplete, but then I will know everything completely, just as God now knows me completely.

1 Corinthians 13:11-12 nlt

I will instruct you and teach you
in the way you should go;
I will counsel you with my loving eye on you.

Psalm 32:8 niv

God's solid foundation stands firm, sealed with this inscription: "The Lord knows those who are his."

2 Timothy 2:19 niv

Joy

You will go out in joy

and be led forth in peace;

the mountains and hills

will burst into song before you,

and all the trees of the field

will clap their hands.

Isaiah 55:12 niv

Until now you have not asked for anything

in my name. Ask and you will receive,

and your joy will be complete.

John 16:24 niv

Satisfy us in the morning with your unfailing love,

that we may sing for joy and be glad all our days.

Psalm 90:14 niv

I have told you this so that my joy may be in you
and that your joy may be complete.

JOHN 15:11 NIV

Be truly glad. There is wonderful joy ahead.... You love
him even though you have never seen him. Though
you do not see him now, you trust him; and you
rejoice with a glorious, inexpressible joy.

1 PETER 1:6, 8 NLT

Let all those rejoice who put their trust in You;
Let them ever shout for joy, because You defend them;
Let those also who love Your name
Be joyful in You.

PSALM 5:11 NKJV

Our mouth was filled with laughter,
and our tongue with shouts of joy.

PSALM 126:2 ESV

Justice

He did not retaliate when he was insulted,
nor threaten revenge when he suffered.
He left his case in the hands of God,
who always judges fairly.

1 Peter 2:23 nlt

He will not break the bruised reed, nor quench
the dimly burning flame. He will encourage the
fainthearted, those tempted to despair. He will see
full justice given to all who have been wronged.

Isaiah 42:3 tlb

Beloved, do not avenge yourselves,
but rather give place to wrath; for it is written,
"Vengeance is Mine, I will repay," says the Lord.

Romans 12:19 nkjv

He will not judge by appearance, false evidence,
or hearsay, but will defend the poor and the exploited.
He will rule against the wicked who oppress them. For
he will be clothed with fairness and with truth.

ISAIAH 11:3–5 TLB

The LORD secures justice for the poor
and upholds the cause of the needy.

PSALM 140:12 NIV

LORD, you know the hopes of the helpless.
Surely you will hear their cries and comfort them.
You will bring justice to the orphans and the oppressed,
so mere people can no longer terrify them.

PSALM 10:17–18 NLT

Righteousness and justice
are the foundation of Your throne.

PSALM 89:14 NKJV

Kindness

He tends his flock like a shepherd:
He gathers the lambs in his arms
and carries them close to his heart;
he gently leads those that have young.

Isaiah 40:11 niv

I am sure that neither death nor life, nor angels nor
rulers, nor things present nor things to come, nor
powers, nor height nor depth, nor anything else in all
creation, will be able to separate us from the love of
God in Christ Jesus our Lord.

Romans 8:38–39 esv

The LORD directs the steps of the godly.

He delights in every detail of their lives.

Though they stumble, they will never fall,

for the LORD holds them by the hand.

PSALM 37:23–24 NLT

You're blessed when you feel you've lost

what is most dear to you. Only then can you

be embraced by the One most dear to you.

MATTHEW 5:4 MSG

Do not let your adorning be external—

the braiding of hair and the putting on of gold

jewelry, or the clothing you wear—but let your

adorning be the hidden person of the heart with

the imperishable beauty of a gentle and quiet spirit,

which in God's sight is very precious.

1 PETER 3:3-4 ESV

Life

I am the resurrection and the life. He who believes in
Me, though he may die, he shall live.

JOHN 11:25 NKJV

Dear friend, listen well to my words;
tune your ears to my voice.
Keep my message in plain view at all times.
Concentrate! Learn it by heart!
Those who discover these words live,
really live; body and soul....
Keep vigilant watch over your heart;
that's where life starts.

PROVERBS 4:20–23 MSG

Sin...doesn't, have a chance in competition with
the aggressive forgiveness we call *grace*.
When it's sin versus grace, grace wins hands down.
All sin can do is threaten us with death....
Grace...invites us into life—a life that goes on and
on and on, world without end.

ROMANS 5:20–21 MSG

We're not giving up. How could we! Even though on
the outside it often looks like things are falling apart
on us, on the inside, where God is making new life,
not a day goes by without his unfolding grace.

2 CORINTHIANS 4:16 MSG

I am the Light of the world; he who follows
Me will not walk in the darkness,
but will have the Light of life.

JOHN 8:12 NASB

Love

We have come to know and have believed the love
which God has for us. God is love, and the one who
abides in love abides in God, and God abides in him.
We love, because He first loved us.

1 John 4:16, 19 nasb

You, O Lord, are good and forgiving,
abounding in steadfast love to all who call upon you.

Psalm 86:5 esv

Know therefore that the Lord your God is God;
he is the faithful God, keeping his covenant of love
to a thousand generations of those who love him
and keep his commandments.

Deuteronomy 7:9 niv

Three things will last forever—faith, hope, and love—
and the greatest of these is love.

1 CORINTHIANS 13:13 NLT

Let love and faithfulness never leave you;
bind them around your neck,
write them on the tablet of your heart.

PROVERBS 3:3 NIV

I will sing of the LORD's great love forever;
with my mouth I will make your faithfulness known
through all generations.
I will declare that your love stands firm forever,
that you have established your faithfulness
in heaven itself.

PSALM 89:1–2 NIV

The steadfast love of the LORD never ceases;
his mercies never come to an end;
they are new every morning;
great is your faithfulness.

LAMENTATIONS 3:22–23 ESV

Nourishment

My God shall supply all your needs according to His riches in glory by Christ Jesus.

PHILIPPIANS 4:19 NKJV

Abide in Me, and I in you. As the branch cannot bear fruit of itself, unless it abides in the vine, neither can you, unless you abide in Me. "I am the vine, you are the branches. He who abides in Me, and I in him, bears much fruit; for without Me you can do nothing."

JOHN 15:4-5 NKJV

Jesus said to them, "I am the bread of life; whoever comes to me shall not hunger, and whoever believes in me shall never thirst."

JOHN 6:35 ESV

Happy are those

who do not follow the advice of the wicked,

or take the path that sinners tread,

or sit in the seat of scoffers;

but their delight is in the law of the LORD,

and on his law they meditate day and night.

They are like trees

planted by streams of water,

which yield their fruit in its season,

and their leaves do not wither.

In all that they do, they prosper.

PSALM 1:1-3 NRSV

My nourishment comes from doing the will of God,

who sent me, and from finishing his work.

JOHN 4:34 NLT

Peace

Peace I leave with you; my peace I give you. I do not give to you as the world gives. Do not let your hearts be troubled and do not be afraid.

JOHN 14:27 NIV

These things I have spoken to you, so that in Me you may have peace. In the world you have tribulation, but take courage; I have overcome the world.

JOHN 16:33 NASB

The LORD will give strength to His people; The LORD will bless His people with peace.

PSALM 29:11 NKJV

If people's thinking is controlled by the sinful self, there is death. But if their thinking is controlled by the Spirit, there is life and peace.

ROMANS 8:6 NCV

God is not a God of confusion but of peace.

1 CORINTHIANS 14:33 NASB

Let the peace of Christ rule in your hearts, since as members of one body you were called to peace.

COLOSSIANS 3:15 NIV

Those who love your instructions have great peace and do not stumble.

PSALM 119:165 NLT

May the Lord of peace himself give you peace at all times and in every way. The Lord be with all of you.

2 THESSALONIANS 3:16 NIV

Perseverance

Consider it pure joy...whenever you face trials of many
kinds, because you know that the testing of your faith
develops perseverance. Let perseverance finish its
work so that you may be mature and complete, not
lacking anything.

JAMES 1:2–4 NIV

God blesses those who patiently endure testing and
temptation. Afterward they will receive the crown of
life that God has promised to those who love him.

JAMES 1:12 NLT

Let us not grow weary of doing good, for in due
season we will reap, if we do not give up.

GALATIANS 6:9 ESV

Wait on the LORD;
Be of good courage,
And He shall strengthen your heart;
Wait, I say, on the LORD!

PSALM 27:14 NKJV

Since we are surrounded by such a great cloud of
witnesses, let us throw off everything that hinders
and the sin that so easily entangles. And let us run
with perseverance the race marked out for us,
fixing our eyes on Jesus....so that you will
not grow weary and lose heart.

HEBREWS 12:1–3 NIV

May the Lord direct your hearts into God's love
and Christ's perseverance.

2 THESSALONIANS 3:5 NIV

The one who endures to the end will be saved.

MATTHEW 24:13 ESV

Prayer

I call on you, My God, for you will answer me;

turn your ear to me and hear my prayer.

PSALM 17:6 NIV

Ask and it will be given to you; seek and you will

find; knock and the door will be opened to you. For

everyone who asks receives; he who seeks finds; and

to him who knocks, the door will be opened.

MATTHEW 7:7–8 NIV

My voice You shall hear in the morning, O LORD;

In the morning I will direct it to You,

And I will look up.

PSALM 5:3 NKJV

Pray without ceasing.

1 THESSALONIANS 5:17 NKJV

The prayer of a righteous person is
powerful and effective.

JAMES 5:16 NIV

The Spirit also helps our weakness; for we do not
know how to pray as we should, but the Spirit Himself
intercedes for us with groanings too deep for words.

ROMANS 8:26 NASB

You, God, are my God,
earnestly I seek you;
I thirst for you,
my whole being longs for you,
in a dry and parched land
where there is no water.

PSALM 63:1 NIV

With all prayer and petition pray at all times in the
Spirit, and with this in view, be on the alert with all
perseverance and petition for all the saints.

EPHESIANS 6:18 NASB

Protection

If you make the LORD your refuge,

if you make the Most High your shelter,

no evil will conquer you;

no plague will come near your home.

For he will order his angels

to protect you wherever you go.

PSALM 91:9–11 NLT

The LORD himself goes before you and will be with you;

he will never leave you nor forsake you.

DEUTERONOMY 31:8 NIV

The Lord is faithful, and he will

strengthen you and protect you.

2 THESSALONIANS 3:3 NIV

How great is the goodness
you have stored up for those who fear you.
You lavish it on those who come to you for protection,
blessing them before the watching world.

Psalm 31:19 NLT

The LORD will keep you from all harm—
he will watch over your life;
the LORD will watch over your coming and going
both now and forevermore.

Psalm 121:7–8 NIV

But let all who take refuge in you be glad;
let them ever sing for joy.
Spread your protection over them,
that those who love your name may rejoice in you.

Psalm 5:11 NIV

But you, LORD, do not be far from me.
You are my strength; come quickly to help me.

Psalm 22:19 NIV

Provision

If any of you lacks wisdom, you should ask God,
who gives generously to all without finding fault,
and it will be given to you.

JAMES 1:5 NIV

May He give you the power to accomplish all
the good things your faith prompts you to do.

2 THESSALONIANS 1:11 NLT

We are God's handiwork, created in Christ Jesus
to do good works, which God prepared in advance
for us to do.

EPHESIANS 2:10 NIV

All scripture is inspired by God and is useful for teaching, for reproof, for correction, and for training in righteousness, so that everyone who belongs to God may be proficient, equipped for every good work.

2 TIMOTHY 3:16–17 NRSV

Then the LORD reached out his hand and touched my mouth and said to me, "I have put my words in your mouth."

JEREMIAH 1:9 NIV

So then, my beloved, just as you have always obeyed, not as in my presence only, but now much more in my absence, work out your salvation with fear and trembling; for it is God who is at work in you, both to will and to work for His good pleasure.

PHILIPPIANS 2:12-13 NASB

Purity

Teach me your ways, O LORD,

that I may live according to your truth!

Grant me purity of heart,

so that I may honor you.

PSALM 86:11 NLT

Now that you have purified yourselves by obeying the
truth so that you have sincere love for each other, love
one another deeply, from the heart.

1 PETER 1:22 NIV

Our faces, then, are not covered. We all show the
Lord's glory, and we are being changed to be like him.
This change in us brings ever greater glory, which
comes from the Lord, who is the Spirit.

2 CORINTHIANS 3:18 NCV

To do what is right and just

is more acceptable to the LORD than sacrifice.

PROVERBS 21:3 NIV

Examine everything carefully; hold fast to that which

is good; abstain from every form of evil.

1 THESSALONIANS 5:21-22 NASB

Whatever is true, whatever is honorable, whatever is

just, whatever is pure, whatever is lovely, whatever

is commendable, if there is any excellence, if there is

anything worthy of praise, think about these things.

PHILIPPIANS 4:8 ESV

Do everything without grumbling or arguing, so that

you may become blameless and pure, "children of God

without fault in a warped and crooked generation."

Then you will shine among them like stars in the sky

as you hold firmly to the word of life.

PHILIPPIANS 2:14–16 NIV

Purpose

You are a chosen people, a royal priesthood, a holy
nation, God's special possession, that you may declare
the praises of him who called you out of darkness into
his wonderful light.

1 PETER 2:9 NIV

We know that all things work together for good to
those who love God, to those who are the called
according to His purpose.

ROMANS 8:28 NKJV

There is a time for everything,
and everything on earth has its special season.

ECCLESIASTES 3:1 NCV

How blessed is God!… Long before he laid down earth's foundations, he had us in mind, had settled on us as the focus of his love, to be made whole and holy by his love. Long, long ago he decided to adopt us into his family through Jesus Christ. (What pleasure he took in planning this!) He wanted us to enter into the celebration of his lavish gift-giving by the hand of his beloved Son.

EPHESIANS 1:3–6 MSG

Confirm God's invitation to you, his choice of you. Don't put it off; do it now. Do this, and you'll have your life on a firm footing.

2 PETER 1:10–11 MSG

No eye has seen, no ear has heard,
and no mind has imagined
what God has prepared
for those who love him.

1 CORINTHIANS 2:9 NLT

Quiet

Why, my soul, are you downcast?
Why so disturbed within me?
Put your hope in God,
for I will yet praise him,
my Savior and my God.

PSALM 42:11 NIV

Pursue a righteous life—a life of wonder, faith, love,
steadiness, courtesy. Run hard and fast in the faith.
Seize the eternal life, the life you were called to,
the life you so fervently embraced in the presence
of so many witnesses.

1 TIMOTHY 6:11–12 MSG

Be glad for all God is planning for you.

Be patient in trouble, and prayerful always.

ROMANS 12:12 TLB

Do not tremble; do not be afraid.

Did I not proclaim my purposes for you long ago?

You are my witnesses—is there any other God?

No! There is no other Rock—not one!

ISAIAH 44:8 NLT

Until the Spirit is poured upon us from on high,

and the wilderness becomes a fruitful field,

and the fruitful field is deemed a forest.

Then justice will dwell in the wilderness,

and righteousness abide in the fruitful field.

The effect of righteousness will be peace,

and the result of righteousness,

quietness and trust forever.

My people will abide in a peaceful habitation,

in secure dwellings, and in quiet resting places.

ISAIAH 32:15-18 ESV

Reconciliation

We have stopped evaluating others from a human point of view. At one time we thought of Christ merely from a human point of view. How differently we know him now! This means that anyone who belongs to Christ has become a new person. The old life is gone; a new life has begun! And all of this is a gift from God, who brought us back to himself through Christ. And God has given us this task of reconciling people to him.

2 CORINTHIANS 5:16–18 NLT

We are made right with God by placing our faith
in Jesus Christ. And this is true for everyone who
believes, no matter who we are. For everyone has
sinned; we all fall short of God's glorious standard.
Yet God, with undeserved kindness, declares that we
are righteous. He did this through Christ Jesus when
he freed us from the penalty for our sins.

ROMANS 3:22–24 NLT

You were separate from Christ...foreigners to the
covenants of the promise, without hope and without
God in the world. But now in Christ Jesus you who
once were far away have been brought near by the
blood of Christ.

EPHESIANS 2:12–13 NIV

Redemption

By entering through faith into what God has always
wanted to do for us—set us right with him, make us
fit for him—we have it all together with God because
of our Master Jesus. And that's not all: We throw
open our doors to God and discover at the same
moment that he has already thrown open his door to
us. We find ourselves standing where we always hoped
we might stand—out in the wide open spaces of God's
grace and glory, standing tall and shouting our praise.

ROMANS 5:1–2 MSG

Be gracious to me, O God,

according to Your lovingkindness;

According to the greatness of Your compassion

blot out my transgressions.

PSALM 51:1 NASB

Once you were dead because of your disobedience
and your many sins.... All of us used to live that way,
following the passionate desires and inclinations of
our sinful nature. By our very nature we were subject
to God's anger, just like everyone else. But God is so
rich in mercy, and he loved us so much, that even
though we were dead because of our sins, he gave us
life when he raised Christ from the dead.

EPHESIANS 2:1, 3–5 NLT

Refreshment

Your love, LORD, reaches to the heavens,

your faithfulness to the skies.

Your righteousness is like the highest mountains,

your justice like the great deep.

You, LORD, preserve both people and animals.

How priceless is your unfailing love, O God!

People take refuge in the shadow of your wings.

They feast on the abundance of your house;

you give them drink from your river of delights.

For with you is the fountain of life;

in your light we see light.

PSALM 36:5–9 NIV

The law of the LORD is perfect,

refreshing the soul.

The statutes of the LORD are trustworthy,

making wise the simple.

PSALM 19:7 NIV

Jesus replied that people soon became thirsty again
after drinking this water. "But the water I give them,"
he said, "becomes a perpetual spring within them,
watering them forever with eternal life."

JOHN 4:13-14 TLB

A generous person will prosper;

whoever refreshes others will be refreshed.

PROVERBS 11: 25 NIV

Jesus stood and said..."Let anyone who is thirsty
come to me and drink. Whoever believes in me,
as Scripture has said, rivers of living water will
flow from within them."

JOHN 7:37–38 NIV

Relaxation

Blessed is the one who trusts in the LORD,
whose confidence is in him.
They will be like a tree planted by the water
that sends out its roots by the stream.
It does not fear when heat comes;
its leaves are always green.
It has no worries in a year of drought
and never fails to bear fruit.

JEREMIAH 17:7–8 NIV

Give your entire attention to what God is doing right now, and don't get worked up about what may or may not happen tomorrow. God will help you deal with whatever hard things come up when the time comes.

MATTHEW 6:34 MSG

Let not your heart be troubled; you believe in God, believe also in Me. In My Father's house are many mansions.... I go to prepare a place for you. And if I go and prepare a place for you, I will come again and receive you to Myself; that where I am, there you may be also.

JOHN 14:1-3 NKJV

Those who love me, I will deliver;
I will protect those who know my name.
When they call to me, I will answer them;
I will be with them in trouble,
I will rescue them and honor them.

PSALM 91:14-15 NRSV

Relief

Come to me, all you who are weary and burdened, and
I will give you rest. Take my yoke upon you and learn
from me, for I am gentle and humble in heart, and
you will find rest for your souls.

MATTHEW 11:28–29 NIV

The Spirit helps us in our weakness. We do not know
what we ought to pray for, but the Spirit himself
intercedes for us through wordless groans. And he
who searches our hearts knows the mind of the Spirit,
because the Spirit intercedes for God's people in
accordance with the will of God.

ROMANS 8:26–27 NIV

I am the Alpha and the Omega—the Beginning and
the End. To all who are thirsty I will give freely from
the springs of the water of life.

REVELATION 21:6 NLT

I prayed to the LORD, and he answered me.
He freed me from all my fears.
Those who look to him for help will be radiant with joy.

PSALM 34:4–5 NLT

Those who sow in tears
shall reap with shouts of joy!

PSALM 126:5 ESV

If you will humble yourselves under the mighty hand
of God, in his good time he will lift you up.

1 PETER 5:6 TLB

Renewal

Praise the LORD!

Oh, give thanks to the LORD, for He is good!

For His mercy endures forever.

PSALM 106:1 NKJV

God put the world square with himself through the
Messiah, giving the world a fresh start by offering
forgiveness of sins. God has given us the task of
telling everyone what he is doing. We're Christ's
representatives. God uses us to persuade men and
women to drop their differences and enter into God's
work of making things right between them. We're
speaking for Christ himself now: Become friends with
God; he's already a friend with you.

2 CORINTHIANS 5:19–20 MSG

We shall not all sleep, but we shall all be changed.

1 Corinthians 15:51 nkjv

The Lord is good to all,
and his mercy is over all that he has made.

Psalm 145:9 esv

If anyone is in Christ, he is a new creation;
old things have passed away;
behold, all things have become new.

2 Corinthians 5:17 nkjv

When you were stuck in your old sin-dead life, you were incapable of responding to God. God brought you alive—right along with Christ! Think of it! All sins forgiven, the slate wiped clean, that old arrest warrant canceled and nailed to Christ's cross.

Colossians 2:13 msg

Restoration

He has saved us and called us to a holy life—
not because of anything we have done
but because of his own purpose and grace.

2 TIMOTHY 1:9 NIV

Dear brothers and sisters, we can boldly enter
heaven's Most Holy Place because of the blood of
Jesus. By his death, Jesus opened a new and life-
giving way through the curtain into the Most Holy
Place. And since we have a great High Priest who rules
over God's house, let us go right into the presence of
God with sincere hearts fully trusting him.

HEBREWS 10:19–22 NLT

Since we have been made right in God's sight by faith, we have peace with God because of what Jesus Christ our Lord has done for us. Because of our faith, Christ has brought us into this place of undeserved privilege where we now stand, and we confidently and joyfully look forward to sharing God's glory.

ROMANS 5:1–2 NLT

Let us praise the Lord, the God of Israel,
because he has come to help his people
and has given them freedom.
He has given us a powerful Savior.

LUKE 1:68-69 NCV

Reward

I have fought the good fight, I have finished the
course, I have kept the faith; in the future there
is laid up for me the crown of righteousness,
which the Lord, the righteous Judge, will award
to me on that day; and not only to me, but also
to all who have loved His appearing.

2 Timothy 4:7-8 nasb

Do not lose the courage you had in the past, which
has a great reward. You must hold on, so you can do
what God wants and receive what he has promised.

Hebrews 10:35–36 ncv

Without faith it is impossible to please God, because anyone who comes to him must believe that he exists and that he rewards those who earnestly seek him.

HEBREWS 11:6 NIV

Watch yourselves, so that you may not lose what we have worked for, but may win a full reward.

2 JOHN 1:8 ESV

Look, I am coming soon! My reward is with me, and I will give to each person according to what they have done.

REVELATION 22:12 NIV

Work with enthusiasm, as though you were working for the Lord rather than for people. Remember that the Lord will reward each one of us for the good we do.

EPHESIANS 6:7–8 NLT

Royalty

As many as received Him,

to them He gave the right

to become children of God,

even to those who believe in His name.

JOHN 1:12 NASB

Love your enemies, do good to them,

and lend to them without expecting

to get anything back.

Then your reward will be great,

and you will be children of the Most High.

LUKE 6:35 NIV

See what great love the Father has lavished on us,
that we should be called children of God!
And that is what we are! The reason the world
does not know us is that it did not know him.
Dear friends, now we are children of God,
and what we will be has not yet been made known.
But we know that when Christ appears,
we shall be like him, for we shall see him as he is.

1 JOHN 3:1-2 NIV

Because we are his children, God has sent the Spirit
of his Son into our hearts, prompting us to call out,
"Abba, Father." Now you are no longer a slave but
God's own child. And since you are his child,
God has made you his heir.

GALATIANS 4:6-7 NLT

Safety

The LORD also will be a refuge for the oppressed,

A refuge in times of trouble.

Those who know Your name

will put their trust in You;

For You, LORD, have not forsaken those who seek You.

PSALM 9:9–10 NKJV

The name of the LORD is a strong tower;

The righteous runs into it and is safe.

PROVERBS 18:10 NASB

God is our refuge and strength,

an ever-present help in trouble.

PSALM 46:1 NIV

Taste and see that the LORD is good;

blessed is the one who takes refuge in him.

PSALM 34:8 NIV

Wherever I am, though far away at the ends of the

earth, I will cry to you for help. When my heart

is faint and overwhelmed, lead me to the mighty,

towering Rock of safety. For you are my refuge, a high

tower where my enemies can never reach me.

PSALM 61:2-3 TLB

I look for someone to come and help me,

but no one gives me a passing thought.

No one will help me;

no one cares a bit what happens to me.

Then I pray to you, O LORD.

I say, "You are my place of refuge.

You are all I really want in life."

PSALM 142:4-5 TLB

Satisfaction

Because your love is better than life,

my lips will glorify you.

I will praise you as long as I live,

and in your name I will lift up my hands.

I will be fully satisfied as with the richest of foods;

with singing lips my mouth will praise you.

PSALM 63:3–5 NIV

Give, and it will be given to you.

A good measure, pressed down, shaken together

and running over, will be poured into your lap.

For with the measure you use,

it will be measured to you.

LUKE 6:38 NIV

Whoever pursues righteousness and love
finds life, prosperity and honor.

PROVERBS 21:21 NIV

God is able to provide you with
every blessing in abundance, so that by
always having enough of everything,
you may share abundantly in every good work.

2 CORINTHIANS 9:8 NRSV

The LORD is all I need.
He takes care of me.
My share in life has been pleasant;
my part has been beautiful.

PSALM 16:5–6 NCV

The poor shall eat and be satisfied; all who see the
Lord shall find him and shall praise his name. Their
hearts shall rejoice with everlasting joy.

PSALM 22:26 TLB

Security

You are near, LORD,
and all your commands are true.
Long ago I learned from your statutes
that you established them to last forever.

PSALM 119:151–152 NIV

Every good and perfect gift is from above, coming
down from the Father of the heavenly lights, who
does not change like shifting shadows.

JAMES 1:17 NIV

The grass withers,
And its flower falls away,
But the word of the LORD endures forever.

1 PETER 1:24–25 NKJV

The everlasting God is your place of safety,

and his arms will hold you up forever.

DEUTERONOMY 33:27 NCV

When you go through deep waters and great trouble,

I will be with you. When you go through rivers

of difficulty, you will not drown! When you walk

through the fire of oppression, you will not be burned

up—the flames will not consume you.

ISAIAH 43:2 TLB

Our steps are made firm by the LORD,

when he delights in our way;

though we stumble, we shall not fall headlong,

for the LORD holds us by the hand.

PSALM 37:23–24 NRSV

In peace I will lie down and sleep,

for you alone, LORD,

make me dwell in safety.

PSALM 4:8 NIV

Serenity

Let not your heart be troubled.
You are trusting God, now trust in me.

JOHN 14:1 TLB

In my trouble I cried to the LORD,
And He answered me.

PSALM 120:1 NASB

Be still in the presence of the LORD,
and wait patiently for him to act.
Don't worry about evil people who prosper
or fret about their wicked schemes.
Stop being angry!
Turn from your rage!
Do not lose your temper—
it only leads to harm.

PSALM 37:7-8 NLT

Do not be anxious about anything, but in every situation, by prayer and petition, with thanksgiving, present your requests to God.

PHILIPPIANS 4:6 NIV

Cast all your anxiety on him because he cares for you.

1 PETER 5:7 NIV

Trusting me, you will be unshakable and assured, deeply at peace. In this godless world you will continue to experience difficulties. But take heart! I've conquered the world.

JOHN 16:33 MSG

I want you woven into a tapestry of love, in touch with everything there is to know of God. Then you will have minds confident and at rest, focused on Christ, God's great mystery.

COLOSSIANS 2:2 MSG

Be still, and know that I am God.
I will be exalted among the nations,
I will be exalted in the earth!

PSALM 46:10 ESV

Strength

Have you never heard?

Have you never understood?

The LORD is the everlasting God,

the Creator of all the earth.

He never grows weak or weary.

No one can measure the depths of his understanding.

He gives power to the weak

and strength to the powerless.

Even youths will become weak and tired,

and young men will fall in exhaustion.

But those who trust in the LORD will find new strength.

They will soar high on wings like eagles.

They will run and not grow weary.

They will walk and not faint.

ISAIAH 40:28-31 NLT

"My grace is sufficient for you, for My strength is
made perfect in weakness." Therefore most gladly
I will rather boast in my infirmities,
that the power of Christ may rest upon me....
For when I am weak, then I am strong.

2 Corinthians 12:9 nkjv

Be strong in the Lord and in his mighty power.
Put on the full armor of God, so that you can
take your stand against the devil's schemes.

Ephesians 6:10–11 niv

In Your hand is power and might;
In Your hand it is to make great
And to give strength to all.
Now therefore, our God,
We thank You
And praise Your glorious name.

1 Chronicles 29:12–13 nkjv

Stronghold

We have this hope as an anchor for the soul,

firm and secure.

HEBREWS 6:19 NIV

Let your roots grow down into him,

and let your lives be built on him. Then your faith will

grow strong in the truth you were taught, and you will

overflow with thankfulness.

COLOSSIANS 2:7 NLT

See, I lay a stone in Zion, a tested stone,

a precious cornerstone for a sure foundation;

the one who relies on it

will never be stricken with panic.

ISAIAH 28:16 NIV

When the earth and all its people quake,

it is I who hold its pillars firm.

Psalm 75:3 niv

The Lord takes pleasure in those who fear him,

in those who hope in his steadfast love.

Psalm 147:11 esv

There is none holy like the Lord:

for there is none besides you;

there is no rock like our God.

1 Samuel 2:2 esv

The Lord has been my stronghold,

And my God the rock of my refuge.

Psalm 94:22 nasb

Trust in the Lord forever,

for the Lord, the Lord himself, is the Rock eternal.

Isaiah 26:4 niv

Support

Whom have I in heaven but you?

And earth has nothing I desire besides you.

My flesh and my heart may fail,

but God is the strength of my heart

and my portion forever.

PSALM 73:25–26 NIV

The LORD is near to the brokenhearted

and saves the crushed in spirit.

PSALM 34:18 ESV

The Lord stood by me and gave me strength....The

Lord will rescue me from every evil attack and save

me for his heavenly kingdom.

2 TIMOTHY 4:17-18 NRSV

You, God, see the trouble of the afflicted;
you consider their grief and take it in hand.
The victims commit themselves to you;
you are the helper of the fatherless.

PSALM 10:14 NIV

God will never forget the needy;
the hope of the afflicted will never perish.

PSALM 9:18 NIV

Live as citizens of heaven, conducting yourselves in
a manner worthy of the Good News about Christ...
standing together with one spirit and one purpose,
fighting together for the faith. Don't be intimidated in
any way by your enemies. This will be a sign to them
that you are going to be saved, even by God himself.

PHILIPPIANS 1:27–28 NLT

You are my hiding place;
You shall preserve me from trouble;
You shall surround me with songs of deliverance.

PSALM 32:7 NKJV

Sustenance

I fall to my knees and pray to the Father, the Creator
of everything in heaven and on earth.
I pray that from his glorious, unlimited resources he
will empower you with inner strength through his
Spirit. Then Christ will make his home in your hearts
as you trust in him. Your roots will grow down into
God's love and keep you strong. And may you have
the power to understand, as all God's people should,
how wide, how long, how high, and how deep his love
is. May you experience the love of Christ, though it is
too great to understand fully. Then you will be
made complete with all the fullness of life and
power that comes from God.

EPHESIANS 3:14–19 NLT

God is able to bless you abundantly, so that in all
things at all times, having all that you need, you will
abound in every good work.

2 Corinthians 9:8 niv

You're blessed when you're at the end of your rope.
With less of you there is more of God and his rule.

Matthew 5:3 msg

The Lord is my shepherd, I shall not want.
He makes me lie down in green pastures;
he leads me beside still waters;
he restores my soul.

Psalm 23:1–3 nrsv

Trustworthiness

May your whole self—spirit, soul, and body—
be kept safe and without fault when our
Lord Jesus Christ comes. You can trust the
One who calls you to do that for you.

1 Thessalonians 5:23–24 ncv

The Lord is my strength and my shield;
my heart trusts in him, and he helps me.

Psalm 28:7 niv

Those who know Your name will put their trust in You;
For You, Lord, have not forsaken those who seek You.

Psalm 9:10 nkjv

God, the source of hope, will fill you completely
with joy and peace because you trust in him.
Then you will overflow with confident hope
through the power of the Holy Spirit.

ROMANS 15:13 NLT

God's way is perfect.
All the LORD's promises prove true.
He is a shield for all who look to him for protection.
For who is God except the LORD?
Who but our God is a solid rock?

PSALM 18:30–31 NLT

The works of his hands are faithful and just;
all his precepts are trustworthy.

PSALM 111:7 NRSV

To you O LORD, I lift up my soul.
O my God, in you I trust.

PSALM 25:1–2 NRSV

Truth

You desire truth in the innermost being,

And in the hidden part You will

make me know wisdom.

PSALM 51:6 NASB

Truthful words stand the test of time,

but lies are soon exposed.

PROVERBS 12:19 NLT

Let us not love with words or speech

but with actions and in truth.

1 JOHN 3:18 NIV

When he, the Spirit of truth, comes,

he will guide you into all the truth.

JOHN 16:13 NIV

The very essence of your words is truth;
all your just regulations will stand forever.

PSALM 119:160 NLT

Everyone who does evil hates the light, and will not
come into the light for fear that their deeds will be
exposed. But whoever lives by the truth comes into
the light, so that it may be seen plainly that what they
have done has been done in the sight of God.

JOHN 3:20–21 NIV

His merciful kindness is great toward us,
And the truth of the LORD endures forever.
Praise the LORD!

PSALM 117:2 NKJV

Send out your light and your truth;
let them lead me;
let them bring me to your holy hill
and to your dwelling.

PSALM 43:3 NRSV

Understanding

You know what I long for, Lord;

you hear my every sigh.

PSALM 38:9 NLT

My sheep hear my voice, and I know them, and they

follow me. I give them eternal life, and they will never

perish, and no one will snatch them out of my hand.

JOHN 10:27-28 ESV

Blessed is the one who finds wisdom,

and the one who gets understanding.

PROVERBS 3:13 ESV

God is not unjust; he will not overlook your work and

the love that you showed for his sake in

serving the saints, as you still do.

HEBREWS 6:10 NRSV

Great is our Lord and mighty in power;
his understanding has no limit.

Psalm 147:5 niv

For we do not have a high priest who is unable to
empathize with our weaknesses, but we have one who
has been tempted in every way, just as we are—
yet he did not sin.

Hebrews 4:15 niv

As the heavens are higher than the earth,
So are My ways higher than your ways
And My thoughts higher than your thoughts.

Isaiah 55:9 nasb

Your Father knows what you need before you ask Him.

Matthew 6:8 nasb

Our purpose is to please God, not people. He alone
examines the motives of our hearts.

1 Thessalonians 2:4 nlt

Victory

Can anything ever separate us from Christ's love?
Does it mean he no longer loves us if we have trouble
or calamity, or are persecuted, or hungry, or destitute,
or in danger, or threatened with death? No, despite
all these things, overwhelming victory is ours
through Christ, who loved us.

ROMANS 8:35, 37 NLT

Commit your actions to the LORD,
and your plans will succeed.

PROVERBS 16:3 NLT

Thanks be to God! He gives us the victory
through our Lord Jesus Christ.

1 CORINTHIANS 15:57 NIV

Victory comes from you, O LORD.

May you bless your people.

PSALM 3:8 NLT

In fact, this is love for God: to keep his commands. And his commands are not burdensome, for everyone born of God overcomes the world. This is the victory that has overcome the world, even our faith. Who is it that overcomes the world? Only the one who believes that Jesus is the Son of God.

1 JOHN 5:3-5 NIV

Thanks be to God, who always leads us in triumph in Christ, and manifests through us the sweet aroma of the knowledge of Him in every place.

2 CORINTHIANS 2:14 NASB

Wholeness

GOD made my life complete
when I placed all the pieces before him....
GOD rewrote the text of my life
when I opened the book of my heart to his eyes.

PSALM 18:20, 24 MSG

He will take our weak mortal bodies and change them
into glorious bodies like his own, using the same power
with which he will bring everything under his control.

PHILIPPIANS 3:21 NLT

For you who fear my name, the sun of righteousness
shall rise with healing in its wings.

MALACHI 4:2 ESV

This is how much God loved the world: He gave
his Son, his one and only Son. And this is why:
so that no one need be destroyed; by believing in him,
anyone can have a whole and lasting life.

JOHN 3:16 MSG

What a God we have! And how fortunate we are to
have him, this Father of our Master Jesus! Because
Jesus was raised from the dead, we've been given
a brand-new life and have everything to live for,
including a future in heaven—and the future starts
now! God is keeping careful watch over us and the
future. The Day is coming when you'll have it all—
life healed and whole.

1 PETER 1:3–5 MSG

Wisdom

Do not be unwise, but understand what
the will of the Lord is.

EPHESIANS 5:17 NKJV

The unfolding of your words gives light;
it gives understanding to the simple.

PSALM 119:130 NIV

Listen carefully to wisdom;
set your mind on understanding.
Cry out for wisdom,
and beg for understanding.
Search for it like silver,
and hunt for it like hidden treasure.
Then you will understand respect for the LORD,
and you will find that you know God.

PROVERBS 2:2-5 NCV

Be filled with the knowledge of His will in all
spiritual wisdom and understanding, so that
you will walk in a manner worthy of the Lord...
and increasing in the knowledge of God.

COLOSSIANS 1:9-10 NASB

Do not let wisdom and understanding out of your sight,
preserve sound judgment and discretion;
they will be life for you.

PROVERBS 3:21-22 NIV

What we have received is not the spirit of the world,
but the Spirit who is from God, so that we may
understand what God has freely given us.

1 CORINTHIANS 2:12 NIV

The wisdom from above is first of all pure. It is also
peace loving, gentle at all times, and willing to yield to
others. It is full of mercy and good deeds. It shows no
favoritism and is always sincere.

JAMES 3:17 NLT